hæmatograms

nigel ellis

NeoPoiesis Press

NeoPoiesis Press

Inquiries:
P.O. Box 38037
Houston, TX 77238-8037

Primary Address:
2775 Harbor Ave SW, Suite D
Seattle, WA 98126-2138

www.neopoiesispress.com

nigel ellis – Haematograms
ISBN 978-0-9855577-4-4 (paperback : alk. paper)
        1. Poetry. I. ellis, nigel

Printed in the United States of America.

First Edition

*"And as we spoke – however gingerly- we knew
the blackbird in our voice, and watched it flying
there, high above the water, until our*

*conversation resembled its illusive song –
though it was the bird that sang amidst the rolls
of thunder…"*

Robert Adamson, "Sail Away"

Contents

dreamhusks

everything
vanishes

vanishing point

(i)

he stops. says he has been waiting.
she smiles.
he asks her where they are going.
she smiles.
says all roads are like this one.

she says she takes her coffee the way
she takes her roads.
he brings her coffee. the dark liquid slips down her
throat
the red tide of dawn flows out towards them,
sweeping through the thin scrub
to break over the low building.
beyond it the heat begins to gather.
he says it is time to move.

if there were bends,
around each would be
a carcasse and crows
there are no bends.
crows are lifted and scattered
as they pass.

he thinks he sees ahead,
at the limit of sight
a kadaichi man

walking on his reflection

singing a thing into being

his feather shoes

rippling the air.

he thinks he hears a bone flute.

the tyres hum with the sound of bullroarers.

he thinks he hears his name.

when they talk they say the same things

in different languages.

she says there is no leaving.

he says there is no home.

their words hang with the dust motes.

the heavier ones

settle with the flecks of ash from his cigarette.

the radio rattles with a sound like irrigation.

fragments of song spray out, and evaporate

when they reach the ears. she turns it off and they listen

as the road spins the wheels and their talk

is plucked out through the windows with the blue

smoke.

now there are bends.

she touches a place on a map.

when he shifts his feet on the pedals

the needles on the gauges

flick like dowsing rods.

he turns off the road, the wheel

light between his hands.

when they stop, the red dust rolls over them.
she writes their names on the dashboard
with a wet finger.

now they can hear the heat
pressing on them with the sound of locusts.

there is a look between them
which neither of them owns.
above them leaves hang blue like blades
and dull chrome bark is streaked with rust.

they share water. the water is warm.
they eat. bread, salt, oil.
after they have eaten
he presses her lips against her teeth with his.
she tastes of olives.
they talk tongue to tongue
omitting the spaces between words
not trusting the air. almost
everything vanishes.

(ii)

there is the sound of water
and the sound of sand.
they walk
towards it through the low grasses
scattering crabs and lifting gulls.

her calves are cuttlebones beneath skin
and the cables that anchor her toes
push bow waves through the white grains.

she stops.
he smiles
and asks her which way.
he knows
which way she will say.
she says
this way and her gaze slides
over and past him. there is
a grain of sand in her lashes and the smell
of salt in his nose. the sand is
a broad ribbon of shot silk under the white sun.

a quick gust raises a nap of grains which briefly
stings
their legs the way a puff of breath through the
nostrils can
sting a lover.
he wants to cut her the way
he can cut water and slide up the face of her
beneath the skin of her
breaking wave
to burst through with both their strengths and
crash back into her.
he can feel this, and certain muscles
flicker beneath his skin in quick rehearsal.

behind them, behind the dunes,
the car waits crouched in the heat and ticking.

they are talking. she looks
now here, now here, while he skips
his sight over her face and darts it
like a tongue into what is between her open lips.
her voice is low and measured, and he uses his
to wedge open sentences so that words flow
and spill and pool. water and sand.

he carries his shoes in his hand. he is
closer to the water than she.
as they walk and talk she is edging them
slowly
gently towards the water. he feels
he can see beneath her bones, and
he smiles with the side of his face that
she cannot see.
small waves spend their strength
hissing up the hard-packed sand to lick
their toes. there is the crack and pop
of breathing holes opening behind each
recession of the sea.
then they are walking through the water ankle-deep.
it is cool, and now he feels the prick
of sun on his neck and face. the water
catches at the cuffs of his trousers, climbs
through threads. later
there will be tidemarks.

ahead is an abutment of rock. molten it has squeezed

and bulged and run

so that it twists and spills like flesh.

they climb.

at the top they sit cupped

in each other, watching the water.

they talk of the past.

they talk of the present.

they talk of the moment.

they talk

of falling.

almost

everything vanishes.

(iii)

they are in the car. they

are on the road.

voices

from the radio buzz.

he drives,

his eyes

drinking red miles through a black straw.

she sits,

her eyes

behind sunglasses and milk-blue lids.

two flies

entered the car with them.

now they write in the voice of

their wings

on the windshield. beyond the glass is

pressure of air

enough to

destroy them.

against the glass, they are safe from

the pressure,

trapped,

and in terrible danger. he

bats at them with the back of his hand and stings

the tips of his fingers beneath the nails against

the glass.

for a moment, the sound vanishes,

taking

the small black bodies with it.

he peers at the dashboard and the car

slides off the shoulder of the road.

he twists

the wheel and the flies

lift

from where they have been hiding

on the black road of two names

winding through

the red dust coating the dashboard.

already a fine down of red
begins to blur the black letters.

she breathes
a deep breath and her head turns a little
towards her window.
she opens
it an inch. two. more.
there is the harsh sound of air
being torn.

he speaks to her
of the flies.
she bats at his words with hers
and a crease appears
on the side of her face that
he cannot see.
she says
she will drive. certain muscles beneath his face
flicker in quick rehearsal
of speech.
he speaks.
she is silent.

they do not need to argue
to argue.

the car is stopped.
he climbs out and walks towards the thin scrub.

he makes red mud with water from his body
and looks out across the red metal heat.
he thinks he sees
a kadaichi man
sitting crosslegged on his reflection
singing smoke into being
his feather shoes
tucked beneath him.
he thinks he hears
flies droning.
his ears roar with the sound of roads.
he thinks he hears his name.

his eyes roll up
beyond the sun and into the red
and then the black.
everything vanishes.

(iv)

the white sun boils red
at the back of his eyes
and crowbars up the lids.
he turns his head and stones burn
his cheek.

she floats and flickers above the road.
she is moving around the car. the car
floats and flickers above the road.
the road floats and flickers above

a reflection of a road.

a reflection of a car.

a reflection of

she floats

and

flickers.

heat squeezes his skull.

he thinks levitation must be a sin.

he thinks

they may be lost.

he says

he looks for himself

among the crowd in

her ears and behind her eyes.

where she looks for herself.

she is too far for his small words.

they

rattle against his teeth and drop pebbled

onto the red sand and the burning rocks.

some are blown back into his ears

with the sand and seeds and feathers.

twisted up

by the screw of dust and wind

which moves like smoke.

if there is a look between them

it belongs to them both.

they are too far to see eyes.

she calls.
her words
drop through the thin air
aquiline
and stop to hover in the blast of heat
above the road.
what is between them
crouches like prey
trying to turn its skin
to stone.

his thoughts are wax melting.
his thoughts are a father
watching a son fall.

his thoughts are a sun
falling
through the red
into the black.

in the black,
everything vanishes.

(v)

the shadow of a low building
sweeps away through the thin scrub.

when he looks down at his feet
he sees feathers.

there is the sound of singing.
he begins to walk.

in

a trick

of perspective
and curves
and the lensing of heat

everything vanishes.

nothing disappears

birdshadows

astragal

open and step.
certain temples have
    a low lintel
    a high threshold

one must
    look down
    bow the head
upon entering it is

a way to honour

cross now.
here is an altar

solstice

there will be a moment

of perfect alignment.

a super-imposition

so complete

that the clockwork universe must

       stop

and not

       proceed

until eternity has passed.

and we will make an orrery.

three joyous haiku

·

flotilla of paper boats
brave little sailors
on a katsushika sea

·

composing haiku
your sea beneath me
we make such tiny movements

·

adrift on an endless sea
i am without fear
storms bring only blue skies

sea triptych

(i)

it is a twisting spine
of shell worn
smooth by water
he rubs it
between thumb and finger
       a thing of water
it was always smooth

it is fluted
  sings to him of seas
  slips
through more time than he has
       he has
he has
eyes to see

it is
between thumb and finger.

(ii)

it is a glowing organ
of glass worn
smooth by water

he puts it
into his mouth
       a thing of earth

it was always sand

it is seaglass

   moves molten in time

   becomes

what it is   he begins

       he begins

he begins to undress

it is

in his mouth.

(iii)

it is a way of looking

      to the sky

moon on one shoulder, full

venus on the other, risen

the sky is bleeding sun

the sea is washing it

           the colour

      the colour

the colour of

breathing   the taste

     the taste

   the taste

of

when he is naked

he begins to swim.

portrait of a girl about to jump

falling

        (through the space between
        two joined hands)

falling is the sweetest

the sweetest

        falling

is the sweetest thing

this ancient song

made new.
your hands
make birdshadows
beat against a wall

our pavilion
its silks and streamers

flutter in the chill
breeze of after - noon
await the still

- pause -

the space between
the indrawn breath of day
the slow sigh of night -

a moment in time
a moment away
a moment

.now.

your hands
make birdshadows
beat against a wall

carnival

another dog
bounds along the sand.
"that one's cute" you say
i pant a little, wonder
if you see my tail wagging

.

your coin-operated hips.
i have change in my pocket

.

making out on the beach
like teenagers
together coming undone

.

my body speaks louder than a carnival barker
i tell it hush
you tell me listen

if I wanted

i could sing you
clean and clear and sweet as
meltwater.
wrap you round my alphabet tongue

i could ribbon
the sound of   you
down my xylophone spine
all snaked and laddered and
lickety-split.

i could speak you
burst you berried
on my palate
whistle you through my teeth sharp
and high.

i could twist   with
my tongue a word rope
for you to dance
across with an umbrella in your hand
and a short short skirt you could turn
somersaults

then jump
i could   catch
you in my arms.
there would be cheers. applause.
there would be wolf
whistles.

five small poems

just there
your scent
i come apart

.

speak to me
use
only vowels

.

your steady gaze
thick in the
space
between us

.

the back of my hand
grazes
your lips flower

.

this
thick
tongue
sweetlike
treacle

three breathing haiku

breathe your life into my o–
these pained and jagged
lungs i gasp my eyes fly wide

.

this resonation of hearts
these blind vibrations
we are open to the sky

.

my lips move when i read you
breathing deep and quick
flesh rises up to meet me

when I am very thirsty

and i kneel between your feet
and drink from you as if you were a cup

and you look down
and i look up
and then you look up

what is that?
if it is not love
what is it?

a small madness

(i)

you do not call
i answer anyway.

lately i have seen many small bodies
the smack of tiny lives ended
on my visor we are both hit right
between the eyes.
also,
vacant cicadas, mummified
lizards, fresh and incandescent
rainbow toadsmears in my path
and once, a fox
which i rode by over the course
of days until it was a fox
in memory only and a haze
of once-a-fox-ness
clouding the green air

(ii)

i would not swim today.

there are bluebottles which
even the seagulls will not eat
and i know the surf
full of their fragments

will drive me outraged, whipped
and wealed

to commit atrocities upon my skin
with handfuls of scouring sand

(iii)

i do not recognise my voice.
others have seeped in
and the white water
bubbles through my brain.

crushes memory.

so there are cigarettes
books
and under pandanus

a bed of rocks
and sleep

(iv)

you spoke to me

of taking heart, observing
the vital aged

the childishness
of a much older lover

as if tiredness were a thing
which could be slept away
kept in lidded eyeboxes
the left luggage of a long trip
parcelled up and labelled
"do not open until Christknowswhen".

i feel not young nor old
rather
too little or too much

so are years tallied

(v)

i weave skeins of ink
to thread
and thread to cloth
stitch with memory a faded
denim still life with oilstains

loose around my hips
and belted with strong
and supple sorrow.
then soft black armour
feathered with
the harsh bark and cough
of many small explosions

the comforting illusion
of movement.

reversion

i take
your fine soft words
from under my pillow

i crush
their smooth warm
fabric against my cheek

i inhale
their sweet warm fragrance their
bodyheat

i gently
rub them against my downy
child's cheek

i taste
and tuck a corner into my mouth
to gum and tooth and

i infuse
my own intimate
scent

i place
them back on their altar

i wait
i wait

da capo al coda

given a certain latitude
can these be called songlines?
hymns for Mercator's spider
poised in the geographic centre of
her blue orb.

she weaves grace-notes through her histories.
sticky strings, with glue-beads of
quaver and breve.

his throat catches at a melody
tangles in the cross-hatched web
of lines and staves.
chokes on the dry black specks.

he feels her
tugging at the corners
of his mouth. this is not
silence.
long fingers move contrapuntal
bracket the refrain.

when I washed our sheets

"And that is all this writing should be then.
The beautiful formed things caught at the wrong moment
so they are shapeless. awkward
moving to the clear.."
- Michael Ondaatje, The Gate in His Head

when i washed our sheets

and made ghosts

of *(there were flowers)* soft pigweed green

of crushed cerise

made ghosts

of *(there was your blood)* vermillion to russet

made ghosts

of the imprints

of the imprints

of the imprints

of the flowers

of our bodies

when i washed our sheets

i washed our sheets

washed our

washed

what greedy senses had
snuffed
                    up
          out
stained
          still
                    with
twisting passion

when i washed

hid us
behind
          white
left us
behind
          white
stained
          white
ghosts/   white /   washed

when i hid my face
behind

when i washed our sheets

when it was almost

when it was soon

such a gift of a dream

i woke to

this morning. such a small dream: i dreamed i woke

in my little flat where i had not lived

for many years.

and it was no longer my flat

and i was not with you, nor you

nor even you,

but with one i have met but do not know

though God willing (and there is no God)

may.

it was morning. we had not slept together,

although i think perhaps the flat was hers and she had

slept

nearby.

still she eased herself astride me and perhaps,

i think yes, perhaps

she smiled

as i did – such a small smile.

there were the bedclothes between us and

i was wearing gloves. No

i do not know why. it was

a dream.

i ran my gloved hands along her clothed flanks. she

did not seem surprised by the gloves

or the hands.

there was perhaps a shaft

of muted sunlight

through old glass of mauve

and mottled. it was a dream and

i cannot be sure.

and the smell of sleep. No,

not of sleep

of rest.

there was the luxury of sheets. and gloves.

and i lay in the luxury

of this dream and then, dreaming,

arose and moved through the

four small rooms.

skimmed my fingers across the kitchen table i had

stripped

and waxed those years ago.

ran those same fingers along the sticky

enamelled stovetop and noted

each small remembered mark

on walls and floor.

swam in the Sea of the Long Forgotten.

i made sure to wake before

the dream could end

so i could carry it with me, with the practicality of my

Ginseng tea, my

cigarettes, this morning,

this early morning sun and shade,

the shush of traffic and the dust
of years swept up.

now with my second cup
of Ginseng tea, my third
cigarette, this pen and page i hold,
with my remaining (gloveless) fingers
i hold
this dream. perhaps wine
would hold it better. perhaps
strong red wine would hold
it better.

Please God (but there is no God)
send me tea
rs and cigarettes and strong red wine.
Yes send me strong red wine
but send me no more dreams until
i am beyond
waking.

all your many gifts to me

"Enclosed within -
our breath, to not
blow out candles
or feed fires"
- Amanda Joy,   Contemplation

these walls
we paper with such care
the better to distinguish
one room from another
            (billowing with our breathing)

these walls
of stones or sticks
stacked like memories or laced
like fingers
            (which hold each other up)

the difference between a cage
and a cupped hand
            (how it is roofed)

the thudding heart
against your fingertips

the confinement of the sky

empty hands
            (a bird is never heavier
            than in the moment it lifts)

water
            (and a cup from which to drink it)

consonance. assonance. dissonance.
            (harmonies)

this door

words
            (the legs round which our ricepaper messages
            are bound for flight)

when birds sing such songs,
how can we not whisper harmonies
under our breath?

all lines are tangents to a curve
        (what is possible)

many songs
from few notes
        (this silence.)

beyond waking

I will woo her with my many faults

and sing her songs of loss to pave the way
and as affection grows i'll prune it hard
as if it were a rose
and i a gardner
then i'll show her where
to dig the bitter root
and how to make
a meal of it

and she will teach me how to grasp
that rod of steel i love that's in her eyes
and take it, beat my back and thighs
til blood runs fresh and stains
in rosy petal shapes the sheets
and twisted coverings
of the pain-filled bed
that we will
make to lie in

and we will measure out our paces
back to back and turn to face the singing shot
upon the count and let fly all our ammunition
dance the measured steps
of chivalry and ugly grace
and we will cut our history
according to our cloth
and tailor all our finery
to classic lines and shapes

and yet it need not
be this way although it was
this way before for each of us
tradition is a hard
and jealous master and we love
to walk the old familiar paths.

today

a black cockatoo

tore holes in the afternoon
with its screaming
painted air dark pinched
a wick of macrocarpus in
two toes
two toes
cracked peace
with its bullet tongue
swallowed hope and let fall
dreamhusks

something was shredded
with its screaming
the song sings the bird
the rough round head
the cortége tail the pocket
handkerchief white flash
breaks the black

the song
sings the bird
the nodding plumes
the lacquered cart the lowered
eyes the bright black boot the slight

            pause

the footfall.

flying ants had
filled the stilldawnair
in drifts.
at touchdown
bodies leave wings
are reborn
from flight into secret
dark places.

the night cloud fell
heavy on the mountain
pressed sound through
perforations of meaning
squeezed
cool green light from
bracket fungus
in the still silvered air.

Catholics have a word for this.
the wet open
ribs
the bright hard
spear
the sucking
chest wound

i walk.

i walk.

tonight,

I have the moon

postcards to a lover

Barcelona

it came from nowhere,
in a steamy irish bar just off Las Ramblas,
your hot flash of fury.
the pint glass like lightning struck the wall
(struck his head, if he hadn't ducked)
showering us with rage and glass
and sticky fluid
black in the red room.
the split-second cessation
of that careless craic.

he up off
into the crowded
catalan night,
and you too
by another door.
"oh Christ" i thought, and left
 to look for my lover
and our friend.

i found you somehow
and dragged you back to our pensión
by the wrist
like a child,
remonstrating over your objections,
while you hung back
like a child.

"what on earth did he say to you?"
and you, too drunk and silly
to answer straight.

locking you in our room i took the key
and went again into the night
to search the streets and squares
in the dark soft spanish rain
for our shell-shocked friend
shaking my head
laughing quietly
loving your
temerity.

Athens

in Syntagma, in the shadow of the Parthenon,
made fearless by my foreign-ness
i stood in a pharmacy
asking haltingly
and somewhat too loudly
for something with which
to treat your candida
while the aged patrons
lined against the wall,
variously nodded, winked, cackled, slept,
scowled, and chewed their gums,
hearing my carefully prepared speech
clatter piece by piece
into the chemist's
cool ceramic mortar.

whereupon he pestled it

into a powder,

and made a paste

using the spittle of those ancients,

while speaking in what seemed

almost oracular fashion *(i could not understand)*.

He invoked the great god Ciba-Geigy,

and produced an unguent

to our universal acclaim.

i crossed his palm with silver

took my lover's gift

and left.

Naxos

in our sight twin pillars,

the remains of Diana's temple.

astride a blubbing scooter

the small roundness of our pregnancy

gently nudging at my back,

in the louvred shade of squid drying

like so much dirty laundry

amid the nagging gulls

we had

although we did not know

our last hurrah.

of all possible treasures of that time

what blind prescience made us

choose to souvenir from our studio

a homely, hand-carved, battered
wooden spoon?

Florence

we did not ascend
to the ballooning crown
of Il Duomo,
sandbagged as we were
by the Child, the stroller
the bags and bottles and blankets.

moored in the square
with the poster sellers
exhausted by our argument
at the station that morning
we could barely rise
to the level
of civilised dispute.
"i'll wait here with her.   you go."
"no, you go."
"no, you."

neither of us was prepared
to leave the other.
that would come later.
earthbound then
we left
in search of refreshment
the Child between us.

...and home again *(a sonnet)*

two years
more or less
since you threw me out.

my bewilderment a small and heavy sphere now
rubbed smooth by constant worrying and turning over
the nubs and spikes of anger worn away, mostly.
compressed by countless heartpump squeezes
the bluster driven out like
air from dough
knocked back.
dense and
massy as a dark star.

"i've got bigger balls than you have", you'd said.

maybe, but mine are harder

outlines

to beat a birdswing of desire against her
fluttered lids
> *head cocked to one side*
> *in an attitude of listening*
> *or to drill a gazy hole and crack*
> *a carapace. a beak. chitin. keratin.*

and cup her tales of when and how
and too
> *some words drawn by a needle*
> *through holes in ragged flesh*
> *dissolve. white ridged scar lips*
> *compress against exit. entry.*

to wake from sleep and dream
to breathe
to write in skin
on bone
> *there was water here*
> *still tidemarks blur the lines*
> *of sentimentary rock. process.*
> *a trans-substantiation of minerals.*

to give   *voice*
to keep *silence*

there is smoke without
> *an impasto of air, the marks*
> *trapped. imprints.*

there is fire within

to never ask for what ought
to be offered

> *fingers beneath skin. a game*
> *of scissors*
> *ink in flesh. parchment. codex.*

to leave a line unfinished
to leave

to turn and turn and turn these
the parameters of reverence

interment

"...just to think it all began
on an uneventful moon..."
- Bob Dylan, Shelter from the Storm

there is a way to take

human remains

> *see how he lifts them*

gently from soft earth

red earth cool earth

> *he handles them so roughly*

lay them

and their ghosts

anew

> *let them lie let them lie*

a votive act

> *in soft earth sleeping*

to straighten

once more

scrimmed thighs

clattered ribs

and fill with hot

sweet tears a skullbowl held

once more

which hands had cupped

to drink from lips

these bones are ours we
cradled them
into rich loam and put
our marker over them
by what right does he
conduct himself
and contort these naked sticks
we drank and threw the cup
and then the earth

and let gaze
fall into wells
where once gaze fell
into such blackless depths
that light and dark were memory
       sshhh we remember we

       remember

then
lay out
soft cloth
washed white wrap
sweet strong
bones
       in darkness. Let them lie.

sing
once more
the low soft songs
sing the sleeper
to dreams

         and do not sing

in
the

lull   *lull*

     the hush *hush*

a bye

    a bye

.

deep places

here are rituals we perform: a tea ceremony,
dried green specks tipped from a paper packet
and boiled water poured over. the liquid soothes
throats parched by silence and
tongues swollen with words not said.

> *reading the scattered dregs*
> *we divine where a river runs underground.*

here are gifts we bring: yes this time also
we have brought gifts. we hide them in mouths
already full and speak carefully around them
while we reconnoitre a landscape
our feet mistrust.

> *when we know how they will be received*
> *we unwrap their porcelain voices.*

here are laws of hospitality we keep: heads
touching, we offer and accept tiny sips
of the oceans we exchanged when we last
stood this way. there is a kind of thirst
that grows with drinking

> *and your eyes*
> *say water, water.*

here are boundaries we observe: standing
on stones in a dry riverbed our legs grow roots

toward an aquifer.

rain is swallowed by sand and slips

between the pebbles we dig to suck.

> *your face is tilted to the open sky.*
> *i want to press my hand to the base of your spine.*

it is said that in times of drought there may be children

born and grown since the last rain who won't believe

water can come from sky.

we talk so much of water,

you and i.

when i leave, your eyes on my back

are the sun, and the rain,

and all things.

three poems for K

i.

we were prisoners

when we met

with guarded habits

and cigarette economy.

light-fingered, I pocketed your name

and held it close

intending to steal from you.

paroled, we met again

in breach of our conditions.

stop, thief

you said

and gave to me a key.

i clasped the handcuffs tight

and swallowed it.

ii.

when i've slipped you on

and i'm wearing you

i feel

my beauty is enhanced

because

you are my jewel

iii.

you were so still last night when I woke

i wasn't sure

you were alive.

i lay against your flank

it was a perfect moment

i lay against your flank and thought

you dead beside me

and me holding you

and you dead beside me

and me holding you

i lay against your flank

and thought

it was a perfect moment.

requiem 1

earth
has tethered this flight –
the sweet loamy smell of us
the picked-clean bones of us
this microbial
disarrangement of senses.

one perfect pinion
sabred
air to ribbons.
one scalpel keelbone
dissected
air to breathing-gas.
one fishhook toe
snagged
tides of cirrus.

the scattered feathers move
to breath
which left the lungs
and won't return
the slow exhale:
the cage of ribs
unbarred, the door
swung wide.

the bones are cast
upon the ground,

the fortune gathered up.
this headstone tooth
has bit us off
this tombstone door
has shut us out

the heavy sky let fall
the parts that could not fly.

fragments

cat's cradle

> the swollen purple
> of constricted circulation.

> the prick
> of thumbs, conscience, etc.

> the blue black
> of venous blood.

> entanglement: (n.)
>> a *snarl*.

fingerpuppet

> you
> point out my flaws.
> i
> insert my middle digit
> into my mouth.
> suck.
> display.

> your fingers
> flick your chin.

> later,
> we hold hands.

insensate

there is a scent
on my fingers

there is a stain
on the bed

there is nothing
between us

riddle

does he close you up inside
his man-sized fist?

does he add grist
to your mill?
am i missed,
did we kill?

do you swallow

his bitter

li'l pill?

diver

surfacing through
greenswell heaving
his netted finds aboard

the deck tilts
nothing ever
washes away.

somewhere
in all these shells must be
the nacre-smothered
irritant
for which he bursts
his lungs.

later, beached,
the tops of his toes raw skinned
by his rubber fishfins,
sand crusts with blood and
wounds are roughly mortared closed.

tomorrow he will open them afresh.

later still
while casting for bait
he is stabbed by memory
of a time when
bright steel was enough

untitled (after Don McKay)

Sometimes a voice – have you heard this? –
wants not to be a voice any longer, wants something
whispering between the words, some
rumour of its former life. Sometimes, even
in the midst of making sense or conversation, it will
hearken back to breath, or even farther,
to the wind, and recognise itself as troubled air, a flight path still
looking for its bird
 - Don McKay, Sometimes a voice (1)

today i broke a word. Snapped it.

pestled it to powder

made a paper funnel, then

poured it into my ear

and after that heard nothing

but

the slurring tinnitus

of radio silence.

the taste of you

i can't get

the taste of you

out of my mouth

eat

and drink

though i may

and christ knows i do

i can't get

the feel of you

off my hands

and i've

scrubbed

til i bled

and touched

everything

i could reach

i can't get

the sound of you

out of my ears

and every song

was our song

remember?

requiem 5

we could not bear
to see the house stand empty

blindeyed
hangdoored

so we
demolished it

brick
by fucking

stone

court no. 3

i wore my glad rags.
well, it seemed fitting.

you didn't show.

how am I to feel about being
jilted at the altar of divorce?

it's like I bury you every morning

within

some brief time after waking

when

i think i hear
you raise your voice

i think i watch
you cross a room

i think i stop

to let…

…and…

…you do not pass by…

later

i will bury you again

five things I don't ever want

i don't ever want
to know
another body
the way I knew yours
the way I still know it
in dreams
and when I see you

I don't ever want
to hear
another voice
say the things i've heard yours say
to me
about me
at different times meant or unmeant

i don't ever want
to have
another child
to feel the distance cut
like a bad edge
on a cheap knife in
one clumsy hand against the other

i don't ever want
to see
another see
you the way I see you

when I look

through the spyglass

of our past and present intimacy

i don't ever want

to be

alone with you without

being

with you.

there is nothing to do

but sleep
the soft bye
cuts

my beaches carved away
now only rocks to walk on
watchtowers fallen into the sea

having decided
that there is no refuge to be taken
in drinks or drugs

after your voice
there is nothing to do but sleep

dreamhusks

water bottle

it has become the custom
among our kind to always carry
water.
it is truly the age of Aquarians
each polycarbonate amphora
spilling greedy
for want of lack.

i embrace parching
wrap it in thick furred tongue
close it in creaking voice box
surrounded by small seas i
drink not.

salt sharpens thirst.
this is the conundrum of oceans.

geograph

i look for words which might elucidate
among my poet friends, their books.
i dogear pages, sit in scattered
mulch of aphorisms and a confetti
of autumnal ennui. i find nothing.

*

here he is.
he is on a mountain.
a road enters a forest, as sure and wet
as any metaphor. in the deep forest
in the night in the
absence of the moon
he cannot see a hand in front of his face.
he must walk with one foot
on the road, one off.
when he sees the sky, the broad ribbon of stars
which might be a road he knows
is not a road. forest and night collide
like metal.
flesh tears. bones break.   the stars are
a lapful of worthless diamonds
and a new red cartography of damage
is already drying on his face.

is there such a thing as direction?
a bare tree is also a symbol for 'river'.

its roots are a delta emptying
into a sea of earth.

in any landscape, scars only remain
scars for so long
before
the habit of long association makes friends of them.

light does not create vision.

*

i have built
i have built
i have built all kinds of structures. some
for living in, others for viewing
from a distance. furniture too, and other
accoutrements such as picture frames
and the things within them. i have etched
haematograms on parchment eyelids:
a kind of invisible ink
to be read
when i lie on my back, face to the sun.
this is the best position for remembering
and forgetting. insects will
enter my ears. mechanical, electric,
on needle legs, their amplified desires will
become the inner groove of meaning and intent:
a comfort of irritation.
i will let the grass grow under me.

*

he has torn
down
everything.

he has torn down
houses, cities, whole civilisations of memory
just so he could fossick
broken-nailed in the rubble
for a perfect stone. he has combed coastlines
and learned to read from sand
the deconstructed histories of continents
mountains, alluvial plains,
petrified forests
bones.

he has torn down his present
and his future.

*

i say
there are two of me. each insists
i prefer the other. he is more…
…synthetic.
we bump shoulders. snigger
at our cleverness. share make-up, raid
each other's wardrobes.

play the twin's game of

open-faced

wide-eyed deceit.

we fool no one. we are too alike.

*

again:

he was in a forest.

he was inappropriate

in dress and manner. his pith helmet

blocked his view of the canopy

until he left it wedged in roots

to gather water, moss,

the brief appreciation of generations

of the chitinous and carapaced

and the fiercely insectivorous thanks of amphibians.

his creased clothing became rags.

he filled the pockets with reminiscences

and stuffed them into crevices.

buttoned a frayed and lonely cuff around a python's neck.

one day, forgot his boots. left them speechless,

tongues hanging out to catch the rain.

discovered

when there are no clothes,

there is no nakedness.

he stopped collecting everything but light
and as for naming? named nothing. forgot
his own. his hair grew.
sometimes he would see glowing
some brief cruel inflorescence of desire
with its attendant nectar-sippers.
he would stare until the perfect colours
ceased to hurt his eyes.

sometimes he was a river.
sometimes he was a leaf. a tooth. a snail.
once, he tripped over a knapsack full of
things he had no memory of forgetting.
once, he spoke
then ran from the sound in fear and shock.

*

there was a period when i stayed silent
for some weeks. I was alone. it was
an experiment. i was alone.
time
became

seamless. it was a meditation.
for day upon day upon day things
only entered my mouth. nothing
left it. i did not write. i breathed only
through my nose. I was alone.

i was in love
with a new
virtue. i was a monk.
a tree. a lake. i was

made to speak. i remember
profound grief in that moment.
naked again, bereft, i re-entered the world.

*

they were saying goodnight.
they walked towards her door.

she was behind him in the hall. he reached back,
took her hands
and laced them on his belly, covered them
with his. their steps slowed.
they were one clumsy creature. he could feel
her breasts,
cool against his back. her hips,
and her mound
a small fire. the serpent's tail.

he did not try to turn. she did not try to turn him.
they reached the door. the night air was chill.

*

there are times when,
seeking relief from symptoms,

i cram my mouth with so much sugar
that my tongue swells. rivers
of it burn my throat until the sweetness
becomes the taste of blood. awareness
at once dilates
and dwindles. is this lust?
there are pills i do not take.

in the mirror, i notice how grey i have become.
in the bed, i cup my cock and balls in my hand.
in the dark, i hear the bright chirp of my phone.

i do not pick it up.

*

he would be a philosopher, if he could.
he would note in the iterations
of water and sand, the arcs of birds and fish,
the circles we must all complete.
he would use our small spheres,
the orbits we trace,
to map with algebraic certainty
the pinwheel motion of our galaxies:
in the ancient light of stars,
the nebulae of our births
the infinitely massive singularities
of our deaths. he would say
i have never seen in a bottle
anything that i have not seen

in a twist of smoke. i have never seen
in a twist of smoke anything
that i have not seen
in a needle, i have never seen
in a needle anything
that i have not seen in some other's face,
or in mine.
he would say
i have never seen anything.

he would say
i have given birth. here is my child.
my mirror.

he would say
when we meet,
parts of us speak. parts of us
are audience. parts of us reach out.
parts of us remain hidden. parts
of us touch.
we eat and drink of each other
and are nourished.

all will be well.

when I was a boy

our house was built by men whose grins were
hard-earned
and hoarded like our pennied pocketmoney
who wielded tools made of
ancient iron and steel
of ancient shapes
ancient sounds

nailing floorboards:
tik (to set the nail)
bangBANG
and two inches of steel nail
driven within a whisker of dead flush
by a sixteen ounce clawhammer at the end of a hard arm
through a hardwood board into a hardwood joist
and not a single half-moon in that floor
or at least not where anyone
would see

in two strokes:
tik (to set the nail)
bangBANG
tikbangBANG
fast, and with a rhythm so precise
you could sleep through it.

sawdust fell like summer rain
from the teeth of the ripping saw

pushed by the conrod arm
and don't touch a man's chisel
a plane brought forth
the fragrant golden curls
of a well-kept woman
caressed the buttery wood
wreathed the hard arms
the ringlets shaken free
their gratuitous beauty unremarked.

and curses were tossed like oranges
in season and cheap, man to man.

and a house grew up
in the time it took a boy
to learn that a man
could love his skills
the way he loved a wife
with open eyes and
a calloused caress

and love his work
with a sharp laugh
and a bedroom tongue

not like it

and not look back.

this boy

has one foot in the air

this boy

sees liminal

this boy

keeps a cricket
in his cupped hands

spies the moon
from his bed

knows where
the small things live

this boy
is not a photograph.

this boy
knows
that boy

this boy

is as long

as the day is wide

this boy

wand

ers

home

for dinner

counterpoint

sing that song
Mother the one
you sing with your blue
with your milk blue
throat so warm and taut
and beating time
and your breast
your breast so curved
and full your belly
my ear to your belly
your breast i hear
such a soft rush
of life of
love..

sing that song
Mother and let
blue milk-crystal
syllables be baubles

strung between

pink fingertips
pink lips pink
nipples

blue milk

sing
mother..

icarus

jumped

flew

      high and caught

the

          su...

             oh

the burning

          sun

            so

          high

    and   caught

(icarus
jumped)

             flew

    oh

so

    high
    and

       caught

the sun

    the   burning

    sun

the burning

sun

there are all kinds of moons

some are just ordinary. slip by.
some are even sweet. gentle.
some are Marx Brothers *F*ire *A*larm *F*rantic
some are harsh enough to

whistle through

the groaning night in a flight
of crystal wind-shard daggers
sharp enough to tear the words
right off a man's tongue
ruin the fine features
blind him

it's been one of that kind.

sometimes i hear the moon coming
from Days away

i hear the moon coming like a locomotive
from days away in the fine tremor in the
dancing dust
i hear the moon coming like a locomotive
and the tracks too stiff and straight and the
steam up
i hear the moon coming like a locomotive
the ragged shriek in the brass throat driven by the
hot blood

i hear the moon coming like a locomotive

and it is *too big*

and its awful heavy speed

too peremptory

its passage tears the world

and from the rent the wounded

spill out

and the great krieglight moon

has ways of making you talk

and the flat *light presses down*

and forces the breath through the body

and the cold *light drains the blood*

and uses it to ill purpose

and the silver *hands slip the halter*

give the thing its head

and the devil take the hindmost

and the great roaring phosphor moon

plucks one up in the bright crashing surf

slips the sand from under one's feet

slips the air from under one's nose

and crams the mouth with

salted *fragments of promise*d breath-to-come-

and *works the limbs* puppet-fashion

calls the steps

for the old dance

and the great magnet moon
that pulls the tides about itself
ruglike as it tosses
and turns will *pull me up*
into its restless dreaming
and *shrug me off* on some far shore
before it turns again

and the great heavy moon
will rest its sad cold weight
in my *arms like a lover*
and brush my cheek
and tell me
nevermind

and leave me.

always leave me
with its promises

it needs a barest breath

see this brimming snailshell beast that grows

its rings imperceptible, careful, slow –

impelled through landscape

by soft flesh over

barren-seeming brick and moss

meadows that must be rich, because

we stop

to graze

it needs a barest breath

to make the eyes flinch

the body curls in

cringing tense of bonelessness

see how we pause and lock –

hold tight and lock, our

edges sealed while we wait blind

for the blow for the burst

door

it needs a barest breath

and we wait on crystalline

paths we wrote

from one meal to the next –

furled tight around the centre of

our meat, anticipating

the jagged

shatter

of our curvature

pastoral, confined

the way you suckled at it all, poor
you
you motherless lamb all
hard palate and nubs of teeth
letterbox eyes grasp of tongue
and the pulse at your neck.

the way you pulled at those
fingers
braced like
your little legs
your empty belly
crawling up your throat
to bleat please –

the way the bell-wether
stood
in a corner of the yard
in a sting of ammonia
ringing the hours
with each dip of her head.

the way the bucket
rang
as it struck the ground
the way the gate latch
clicked

that boy

i know that boy

in that photograph that boy
with the open face

the too-wide smile
the tombstone teeth
the too-small chin

birdmouth open for the camera
a promised gift
a sweet

a sweet someday
that boy knows
so much about so

little

so little

that boy knows

i don't pity
that boy i don't wish
him well or ill

i
don't
know
that boy

i want to
rattle his teeth
that boy and shake
the thin shoulders
that boy and shout
through the songs
that boy sings and
slap some colour and
wipe that smile and
that boy should KNOW

that i don't know
anymore
that boy

misogyny

because i cannot understand
a birth

because i cannot sing
the moon

because i am not
forked

because i may not give
sustenance

because i possess neither the tools nor
the wit

because i must
poke
and prod and stir and stick
and stab and club and swing
the lead
and drag the heavy chained
ball
because i cannot get from under the pawnbroker's
globes
because i
owe

because the cleft is
a gulf

because i may not
cross over

because i must fall

always fall

into the original sea

the salted sea

found poem

every morning
the world tells its name to us

every day
takes figuring out

all over again
how to live

it's the

learnin nothin
that keeps me

young

- lines in episodes of the HBO drama series "DEADWOOD"

parable

and on the dusty ground a snowy cloth
its warp and weft as tight and thick
as lover's moonlit words
and bleached whitehard, and napped and ironed
across the eaten holes and fraying hem
and odd, three-cornered tears
with darning stitches flat as hammered nails
and glossed by starch
the honest glary face of blinded years
a splash beside the dusted road

and on the dusty ground a vendor squats
and rocks on heels
as cracked as tarmac's blistered path
and grained with souvenirs of roads
as long as winter's close-held tales
and bleak and endless as a wasted life
with face and neck and arms and hands
deep-scored as weathered wood and charred
and droughted, channelled deep by
flooding tears and scarred like landscape far below
the nagging, scudding crow

and past the leathered delta lapped
by sweated salted crusted cloth
untouched by sun or wind is hidden skin
of breasty white and writ with secret runes
of scrawling calligraphic blue

of maps of paths and cul-de-sacs
and journeys without end or not begun
and vistas long since lost to view
and hid from sight the bitter bastard child
named hope when hope is twisted all askew

and on the snowy cloth a single fruit
of varied ripeness and uncertain hue
inflicted here and there with studied wounds
and greedy hungered sucks and bites and bruised
by blows and squeezed by careless hands
a bellied gravid pulpy womb and cradled deep within
and hidden from the worm which writes unthinking
want
between the porous skin and bitter pith
the armoured seed lies blinded deaf and dumb
and waits for ruin's eager laugh to give it voice
and free it from its sugared tomb
to curl and drink the sun or burn or drown

and on the dusted road a host of feet

and in the bone-barred chest a stuttered heart

and on the snowy cloth a weeping fruit

and in the blinding sky a blinding sun

pray

give us this day
our quotidian layings-on-of-hands
and searchings-of-faces

and forgive us not
our manifold indiscretionsour
merry leering weeknesses

for thine is the game
thy bat and thy ball

comfort me

maketh me to lie down

please

for ever
an never

a - hummm
a — hummm

fortune cookie at the last supper

you own rights to
nothing.

you must ask for
everything.

answers
may not be forthcoming.

sleep does not come easily

there are pains and aches
old wounds, losses, lacks
and the terrible work of forgetting

turnings and re-turnings
tossing
the coin that is the cold hard moon

the crowd around the bed
milling, restless
plucking at the covers
with hubbub
and shrill clamour

and always
glacial
implacable
dawn.

sleep does not come easily

city

i will be the gap that one minds.
i will be the blank space
on a crowded wall

i will be the footprints
lost in a maze of others
i will be the air
in a conversation

i will be the cigarette
one must not smoke
i will be
an illicit meal, high
in fats and sugars

i will be every alley
and rat's run
i will be
broad boulevards and
tall buildings

i will be the hole
i will be the city.

diagnosing the human condition

oh, pity

we human creatures

with our jellied brains

and our hard, hard mouths

oh, pity us

we cannot.

su

chsm

allwordsrip

plestillsuchsm

allwordsripplest

illpoolsandpuddlesandmi

ghtyoceanssuchsmallwordsmakesu

chwavessuchtumultsuchsturmunddrangsuchsm

all

w

o

r

d

s

Acknowledgements

Many of the works here have previously been published to the author's blog, <u>Crow Files</u> (http:dorlova.blogspot.com.au).   Some, though not all of these works, are still visible there.   Other works, including but not limited to (i was never much of an accountant), *"a small madness"*, *"requiem 1"*, and *"it needs a barest breath"* were first published in various editions of the Speedpoets 'zine (www.speedpoets.com).   *"if i wanted"* first appeared in print via *Westerly vol. 57, no. 2, 2012.*

I acknowledge the depthless support of my parents Jane & Ed Ellis. My eternal thanks also to Chris & Cathy Ellis; also to Peter Joseph, Frank Walsh, Andrew & Jo Soot-Hurst, and other close family & friends too numerous to mention here.   I have & will spread the love as & when i see you all – you have all helped to make this volume possible.   My profound thanks also to Graham Nunn, and to all the Speedpoets crew.   You guys are like family.   Others may also recognise my interactions with them in these poems.   I thank you all, and love you as i ever did and indeed do still.   I would not be who i am without you.

Ultimately, this li'l book would not exist without the belief, determination, and dedication of Dale Winslow and Erin Badough, of NeoPoiesis Press.   I cannot find words to adequately express my appreciation for their efforts in bringing this project to fruition.

About the Author

nigel ellis is a poet, songwriter and author, currently undertaking a B. Fine Arts with a major in Creative Writing at Queensland University of Technology. He has published in numerous print and online journals, and is perforce currently based in Brisbane, Australia.

NeoPoiesis: *a new way of making*

1) in ancient Greece, poiesis referred to the process of making: creation - production - organization - formation - causation

2) a process that can be physical and spiritual, biological and intellectual, artistic and technological, material and teleological, efficient and formal

3) a means of modifying the environment and a method of organizing the self, the making of art and music and poetry, the fashioning of memory and history and philosophy, the construction of perception and expression and reality

4) an independent publisher with a steadfast goal to print and promote outstanding poets, writers and artists that reflect the creative drive and spirit of the new electronic landscape

NeoPoiesisPress.com